Little Stars

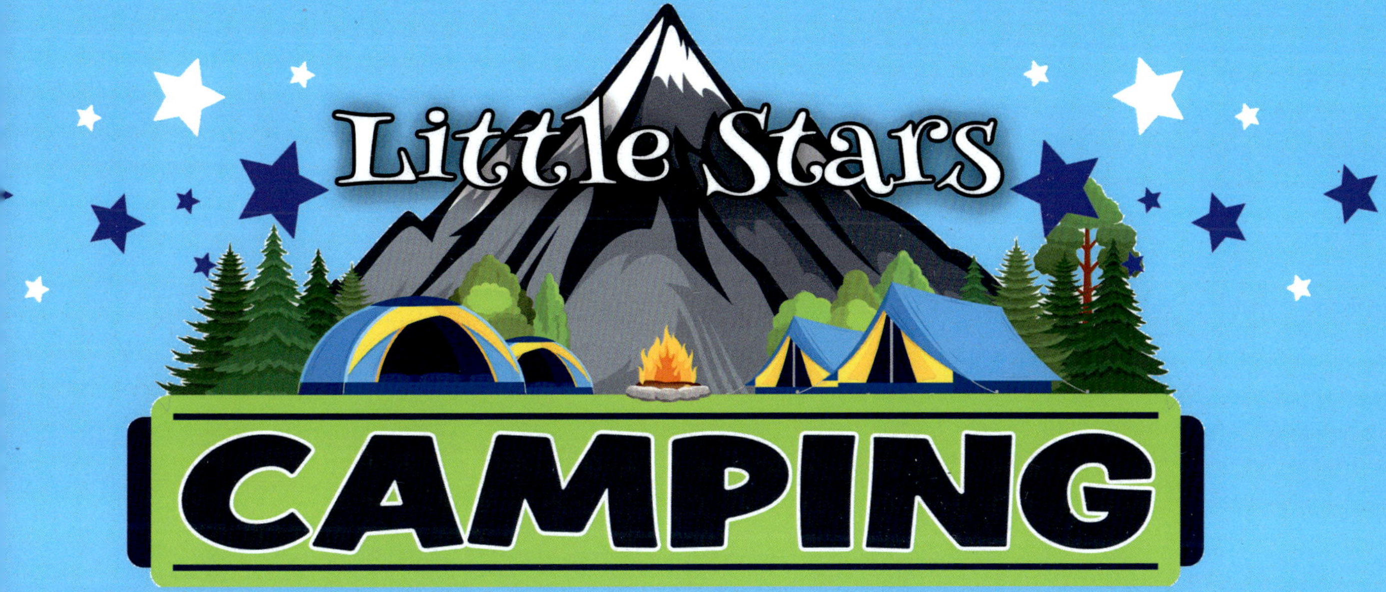

Little Stars CAMPING

A CRABTREE SEEDLINGS BOOK

Taylor Farley

We are at
the **campground**!

3

Let’s set up our tent.

We can go **exploring**.

We can fish in the lake.

Let's build a **campfire**.

We can **roast** hot dogs.

We can roast **marshmallows**.

Nighttime is here.

Let's find the **Big Dipper**!

Time for bed.
Let's get in our tent.

Glossary

Big Dipper (BIG DIP-ur): The Big Dipper is a group of seven bright stars. These stars make a pattern that looks like a handle and a bowl.

campfire (KAMP-fire): A campfire is a fire built by campers. Campfires keep campers warm and can also be used for cooking.

campground (KAMP-ground): A campground is a place where people can set up tents and camp.

exploring (ek-SPLOR-ing): When you are exploring, you are traveling around to find out what a place is like.

marshmallows (MARSH-mal-lohz): Marshmallows are round, squishy candies.

roast (ROHST): When you roast something, you cook it in a very hot oven or fire.

Index

School-to-Home Support for Caregivers and Teachers

Crabtree Seedlings books help children grow by letting them practice reading. Here are a few guiding questions to help the reader build his or her comprehension skills. Possible answers are included.

Before Reading

- **What do I think this book is about?** I think this book is about camping. It might tell us about activities children do while camping. The picture on the cover shows children roasting marshmallows!
- **What do I want to learn about this topic?** I want to learn about the things people should bring with them when they go camping.

During Reading

- **I wonder why...** I wonder why the night sky looks bright and blue.
- **What have I learned so far?** I learned from the words and pictures that people should bring tents, sleeping bags, flashlights, and food.

After Reading

- **What details did I learn about this topic?** I learned that people do many activities while camping. They go exploring and fishing. They roast hot dogs and marshmallows. They look at stars.
- **Write down unfamiliar words and ask questions to help understand their meaning.** I see the word *campground* on page 2 and the word *roast* on page 12. The other vocabulary words are listed on pages 22 and 23.

Library and Archives Canada Cataloguing in Publication

Title: Little stars camping / Taylor Farley.
Other titles: Camping
Names: Farley, Taylor, author.
Description: Series statement: Little stars | "A Crabtree seedlings book". | Includes index. |
Previously published in electronic format by Blue Door Education in 2020.
Identifiers: Canadiana 20200378880 | ISBN 9781427129765 (hardcover) | ISBN 9781427129949 (softcover)
Subjects: LCSH: Camping—Juvenile literature.
Classification: LCC GV191.7 .F37 2021 | DDC j796.54—dc23

Library of Congress Cataloging-in-Publication Data

Names: Farley, Taylor, author.
Title: Little stars camping / Taylor Farley.
Description: New York, NY : Crabtree Publishing Company, [2021] | Series: Little stars: a Crabtree seedlings book | Includes index.
Identifiers: LCCN 2020049392 | ISBN 9781427129765 (hardcover) | ISBN 9781427129949 (paperback)
Subjects: LCSH: Camping--Juvenile literature.
Classification: LCC GV191.7 .F37 2021 | DDC 796.54--dc23
LC record available at https://lccn.loc.gov/2020049392

e-book ISBN 978-1-949354-63-8

Print book version produced jointly with Blue Door Education in 2021

Printed in Canada/012022/CPC20211228

Photo credits: Cover photo © Sergey Novikov, cover art © Vlad Klok; page 2-3 © Hills Outdoors; page-4-5 © LightField Studios; page 6-7 © Monkey Business Images; page 8-9 © AlohaHawaii; page 10-11 © Soloviova Liudmyla; page 12-13 and 14-15 © Hurst Photo; page 16 © Andrey Arkusha, page 16-17 © galsand; page 18-19 © RonTech3000; page 20-21 © natalia_maroz; page 22 top photo © Tatyana Vyc; page 23 middle © Natali Zakharova
All images from Shutterstock.com